Before You React

Why we defend, explain, argue, and fix –
and what happens when we don't

MARCUS NICOLLS

Published 2026

Printed in the United States of America

ISBN: 979-8-9954232-0-1

CONTENTS

OPENING NOTE

Why This Book Is Short

This is a short book because the problem it points to is not complicated.

Most of our suffering doesn't come from what happens to us.
It comes from what we feel compelled to do next.

Someone questions us; we defend.
Someone misunderstands us; we explain.
Someone disagrees with us; we argue.
Someone struggles; we rush to fix.

These responses feel responsible.
Even noble.

But over time, they quietly exhaust us.

The issue is not that we respond.
It is that we often respond before we see clearly.

This book is not here to teach you better techniques for defending, explaining, arguing, or fixing.
It's here to help you notice when you don't need to do any of them at all.

You are not broken.
You are not doing life incorrectly.

You are responding the way most of us were conditioned to respond.

And that conditioning can be seen.

Once it is seen, it loosens on its own.
You don't need more strategies.
You need a little space.

This book offers that space.

Read it slowly.

Put it down often.

Let recognition do the work.

CHAPTER 1

The Reflex to Respond

The moment before you move

Most of us believe that being a good person means responding well.

We listen carefully.

We explain ourselves clearly.

We correct what's wrong.

We help where we can.

But rarely do we ask a simple question:

Why do I feel the need to respond at all?

Someone questions us; we *defend.*

Someone misunderstands us; we *explain.*

Someone disagrees with us; we *argue.*

Someone struggles; we rush to *fix.*

These reflexes are consistent enough to form a pattern.

Between what happens and what we do next, there is a moment – often so brief we don't notice it. In that moment, something inside prepares.

The body tightens slightly.
The breath shifts.
The mind begins assembling language.

We call this engagement.
But very often, it's anxiety.

Not dramatic anxiety.
Not visible panic.

Just a quiet urgency.

Silence feels dangerous.
Not knowing feels irresponsible.
Being misunderstood feels unsafe.

So, we move.

It all happens quickly.
So quickly that we rarely consider whether anything essential is actually at risk.

These responses are reflexes.

They are not moral failures.
They are learned survival patterns.

There was a time this made sense.
Explaining helped you stay connected.
Arguing gave you footing.
Fixing made you valuable.

These patterns worked.
They stayed.

But what begins as protection can slowly become compulsion.

The problem is not that you learned to respond.
The problem is that you rarely learned when not to.

Most of us are over-responding to ordinary life.

We respond as though something essential is always at stake – our worth, our intelligence, our goodness, our relevance.

But most conversations are not trials.
Most disagreements are not threats.
Most misunderstandings are not verdicts.

A conversation is just a conversation.
A difference is just a difference.
A problem is just a problem.

Yet inside, it feels urgent.

This urgency is the real subject of this book.
When it runs the show, we don't choose our responses – we react.
And reaction, no matter how polished, always comes at a cost.

Beneath much of that urgency is not danger, but something quieter.
A fear most of us rarely name – not fear of harm, but fear of being diminished.

The cost is subtle at first.

A slight tension in the shoulders.
A replaying of conversations later in the day.
A quiet need to clarify what no one asked to clarify.

Over time, the cost becomes heavier.

Relationships feel effortful.
Conversations feel loaded.
Rest feels unearned.

And still, we tell ourselves we're simply being responsible.

But responsibility is not the same as reactivity.

There is another possibility.

Not withdrawal.
Not indifference.
Not passivity.

But space.

You don't have to respond to everything that reaches you.

This is not advice.
It is a recognition.

Not every misunderstanding needs clarification.
Not every opinion warrants a counterpoint.
Not every struggle requires your intervention.

There is a moment – before the defense, before the explanation, before the argument, before the fix – when nothing has yet been said.

That moment is small.

But it is real.

At first, staying in it feels uncomfortable.

The mind insists:

If I don't respond, something about me will diminish.

But most of the time, nothing happens at all.

The moment passes.

The tension dissolves.

Life continues.

And something inside begins to loosen.

This book is an invitation to notice that moment – the moment before you react.

Not to suppress it.

Not to override it.

Not to master it.

Just to see it.

When you can see the reflex, you are no longer ruled by it.

And awareness, quietly, begins to change everything.

Pause

CHAPTER 2

Defending

What is real about you does not require defense

Defending rarely announces itself as defense.

It feels like clarification. Like fairness. Like making sure the record reflects what actually happened.

You're in a meeting. Someone questions a decision you made. Nothing overtly critical is said. The tone is measured. But you feel the shift – the slight turning of attention toward you.

Your body responds before your thoughts do.

Your shoulders tighten. Your breath shortens. You begin speaking.

You describe the context. The constraints. The competing priorities. You explain what others may not have seen. You add background information.

You offer nuance. You make sure your reasoning sounds thoughtful.

No one asked for all of that.

But something inside you needed to supply it.

On the surface, you are being thorough.

Underneath, you are protecting something.

Most defending is not about being right.
It's about not wanting to feel exposed.

When someone questions your actions, it can feel as though they are questioning you. And when you equate your actions with your identity, even mild disagreement can register as threat.

The threat does not have to be real.

It only has to be felt.

Perhaps you once learned that being misunderstood meant being corrected publicly. Perhaps you learned that mistakes reduced respect. Perhaps you learned that silence was interpreted as guilt.

So, you adapted.

You learned to explain quickly. To justify preemptively. To anticipate criticism before it formed. You became articulate, careful, prepared.

That intelligence may have protected you.

But protection, when overused, becomes tension.

Defending is exhausting because it never fully resolves the underlying fear.

Even when someone says, "I understand," something remains unsettled. You scan their face for signs of lingering doubt. You replay the conversation later, wondering whether you should have added one more clarification.

The relief is temporary.

Because the real fear was not about the decision.
It was about being diminished.

Sometimes you defend because you are afraid of feeling small.
Sometimes you defend because you fear being seen as incompetent.
Sometimes you defend because you equate misunderstanding with rejection.

That is not weakness. It's history.

But history does not have to govern every present interaction.

There's a difference between offering clarity and fighting for validation.

Clarity says what is true and rests.
Defense continues until it feels safe.

Clarity trusts that truth can stand without constant reinforcement.

Defense assumes that if it stops speaking, something important will be lost.

You can feel this difference in your body.

When you are clear, your voice steadies. Your sentences shorten. Your posture relaxes.

When you are defending, your speech accelerates. Your explanations multiply. You feel compelled to close every possible gap.

What is real about you does not require defense.

That sentence can feel almost reckless.
If you are not defending, are you allowing

misperception? If you do not correct the narrative, are you surrendering reputation?

But reputation built on constant correction is fragile.

It depends on continuous management.

Identity that must be defended constantly is exhausting to maintain.

Consider the possibility that you can survive being misunderstood.
Consider the possibility that someone's incomplete perception of you does not alter what is actually true.

You are allowed to be seen incompletely.
You are allowed to be interpreted imperfectly.
You are allowed to leave an explanation unfinished.

At first, this restraint feels risky. The mind insists that silence will create distortion. But often, when you stop defending, the conversation simply continues.

The room does not collapse.
The relationship does not fracture.
The tension dissipates on its own.

And something surprising happens.

The energy shifts.

When you are not bracing, others often soften. When you are not scrambling to protect your image, the interaction becomes less adversarial. You are no longer fighting a perceived attack; you are participating in a conversation.

This does not mean you never clarify. It does not mean you allow false accusations to stand unaddressed. It means you distinguish between moments that require clarity and moments that trigger old fear.

That distinction is subtle.
But learning it changes everything.

The next time you feel the urge to defend, pause – not to suppress your voice, but to understand your impulse.

Ask yourself:
Is something actually at risk here?
Or am I protecting an image that feels threatened?

That quiet inquiry often reveals more than another explanation ever could.

Over time, defending does something subtle.

It teaches you to live as though you are always being evaluated.

You begin scanning conversations for potential misinterpretation before it even occurs. You anticipate objections. You pre-justify decisions in your mind before anyone has questioned them. Even in neutral exchanges, part of you remains slightly braced.

This vigilance can look like competence.

It can look like preparedness.

But it slowly reshapes your inner life.

When you are constantly defending, you are rarely resting.
And when you are rarely resting, you are rarely open.

Defensiveness narrows perception. It turns conversations into potential threats. It converts curiosity into caution. It makes listening more difficult because part of you is already preparing a response.

Intimacy requires a certain softness – a willingness to be seen without rehearsal.

But when your reflex is defense, you do not feel safe enough to soften. You remain subtly guarded, even with people who mean you no harm.

Over time, that guardedness can become identity.

"I am someone who must stay sharp."
"I am someone who must not be caught unprepared."
"I am someone who must maintain respect."

None of those identities are inherently harmful. But when urgency fuels them, they become rigid.

Urgency drives defense.

Urgency whispers:
This must be corrected.
This must be clarified.
This must be protected now.

But most moments are not emergencies.
Most comments are not verdicts.
Most misunderstandings are not permanent judgments.

Yet when urgency drives your response, every small challenge feels disproportionate.

The nervous system does not distinguish between minor friction and meaningful threat when the pattern is rehearsed enough.

So, you respond as if something essential is at stake. And often, nothing is.

When you begin to see this clearly – not intellectually, but experientially – something loosens.

You realize that not every comment requires correction.
Not every raised eyebrow requires explanation.
Not every incomplete perception requires repair.

And in that realization, defense softens into discernment.

You still speak when clarity is needed.
But you no longer speak from compulsion.
You are no longer fighting to preserve an image.

You are simply participating.

That shift may seem small.
It is not.

It changes the atmosphere of your relationships.

It changes how safe others feel around you.

And perhaps most importantly, it changes how safe you feel within yourself.

Because what is real about you does not require constant protection.

It requires steadiness.

CHAPTER 3

Explaining

Understanding cannot be forced

Explaining feels responsible.

It feels like an act of care. You want to be clear. You want the other person to know what you meant. You want to remove confusion before it turns into distance.

You're at home. A comment you made earlier in the day is brought back to you.

"That's not what you said."

The words aren't aggressive. But they land with weight.

You know what you meant. You remember your intention clearly. And yet, what the other person heard does not match what you believe you expressed.

You feel it immediately – that subtle tightening behind your ribs.

You begin explaining.

You describe what you were thinking at the time. You add context about your day. You clarify tone. You revisit the conversation step by step. You try to reconstruct the moment accurately, hoping that accuracy will dissolve the tension.

You are not trying to win.
You are trying to restore connection.

Because when someone says, "That's not what you said," it can feel like something deeper is being questioned. Not just your wording – but your integrity. Your consistency. Your reliability.

So, you explain.

And sometimes explaining is helpful.
Clarity matters. Misunderstandings deserve attention.

But sometimes explaining continues long after clarity has been offered.

The conversation stretches. The air grows heavier. You find yourself saying the same thing in slightly different language, hoping that one of the variations will finally land.

Underneath the effort is a quiet belief:

If you truly understand me, you won't feel hurt anymore.
Or disappointed.
Or frustrated.

Explaining becomes an attempt to manage the emotional outcome.

You are not just sharing perspective – you are trying to remove discomfort.

Yet understanding cannot be forced.

You cannot think for another person. You cannot ensure that your intention outweighs their experience. You cannot guarantee that your explanation will produce the relief you're hoping for.

Sometimes you explain perfectly and the other person still feels what they feel.

That's when explaining becomes exhausting.

You add nuance. You soften your language. You reassure. You clarify again. You begin to feel slightly desperate for alignment.

It may not look desperate on the surface.

But inside, there is urgency.

Because being misunderstood can feel like being unseen.

And being unseen can feel like being alone.

If you trace that feeling carefully, you may find something older beneath it.

Perhaps you once learned that misunderstanding led quickly to criticism.
Perhaps you learned that clarity was your protection – that if you did not explain yourself thoroughly, others would decide who you were for you.

So, you became articulate.

Careful.

Precise.

You learned to close interpretive gaps before they widened.

That intelligence may have preserved relationships. But it may also have trained you to over-manage perception.

There is a subtle shift that happens when explaining crosses into compulsion.

You stop offering clarity and start chasing relief.

You can feel it physically.

Your sentences lengthen. Your voice speeds up slightly. You lean forward. You feel compelled to fill silence quickly before it solidifies into misunderstanding.

And even after the conversation ends, it continues in your mind.

You replay it.
You refine your explanation.
You imagine a better version – one that would have eliminated the tension entirely.

That rehearsal is rarely about language.

It is about control.

If I can find the perfect phrasing, this discomfort would not have happened.

But the discomfort may not be linguistic.
It may be human.

Two people can experience the same moment differently and both be sincere.
Two perspectives can coexist without one being invalid.

Explaining becomes heavy when it attempts to collapse that difference.

You are not responsible for completing the narrative in someone else's mind.
You are responsible for your clarity.

There is a difference.

You can experiment with that difference.

The next time you feel the urge to explain again – to add one more layer, one more nuance – pause.

Ask yourself:
Have I already been clear?
Or am I trying to control how this feels?

The answer will often surprise you.

When you stop explaining beyond clarity, something changes.

The conversation may remain imperfect.

The misunderstanding may not dissolve completely.

But you remain steadier.

You discover that connection does not require perfect alignment of interpretation.
It requires honesty.

And honesty does not demand repetition.

Over time, explaining softens.
You still speak.
You still clarify.

But you stop negotiating your identity through endless context.

And in that restraint, your words become cleaner – and lighter.

Over time, over-explaining reshapes more than conversations.
It reshapes your relationship with silence.

When you are accustomed to explaining quickly, silence begins to feel dangerous. A pause feels like judgment. A moment without verbal confirmation feels like distance.

So, you fill it.

You clarify before confusion deepens. You justify before accusation forms. You reassure before doubt has even been expressed.

From the outside, this can look like thoughtfulness.

From the inside, it often feels like vigilance.

You are managing emotional climate constantly. And when you are managing climate, you are rarely at rest.

In close relationships, this pattern can create subtle imbalance.

If you are always explaining, you are always adjusting yourself in response to perceived reaction. You become slightly over-responsible for how the interaction feels. You may even begin to assume responsibility for how the other person processes their own emotions.

That creates a quiet pressure.

It can make you attentive – but it can also make you anxious.

Over time, you may begin to distrust your first expression. You may pre-edit yourself mid-sentence. You may soften opinions automatically. You may hedge clarity with disclaimers.

Not because you lack conviction.
But because you fear the rupture of being misheard.

And underneath that fear is urgency.

Urgency says:

Fix this before it escalates.
Clarify this before it fractures.
Explain this before it becomes something larger.

When urgency governs explaining, you do not leave space for ambiguity to settle on its own.

You intervene too quickly.
And sometimes, what needs time never gets it.

The paradox is this:
Explaining in pursuit of perfect understanding can

actually reduce the depth of connection. Because connection is not built on flawless alignment of interpretation. Connection is built on the capacity to remain present even when interpretation differs.

When you stop explaining beyond clarity, something subtle shifts.

You allow the other person to hold their perception without immediately correcting it. You allow space for them to sit with discomfort without rushing to remove it. You trust that a relationship can survive partial understanding.

That trust feels risky.

It feels like relinquishing control.

But control was always an illusion here.

You cannot engineer perfect comprehension.

You can only speak honestly and let your words stand.

And when you do, something steadier emerges.

You begin to notice that you can survive being misunderstood.
You begin to notice that silence does not automatically mean disapproval.
You begin to notice that connection does not require endless clarification.

Over time, explaining softens into expression.

You speak because something is true – not because you are trying to regulate outcome.

You clarify when it serves the moment – not when it serves urgency.

And gradually, the space between what happens and what you say next widens.

In that space, you feel less compelled.
Less defensive.
Less responsible for managing perception.

More present.

CHAPTER 4

Arguing

Needing to be right is rarely worth what it costs

Arguing often begins quietly.

You're at dinner. The conversation turns toward something political, cultural, spiritual, philosophical. Someone says something you disagree with. Not wildly. Not offensively. Just differently.

You feel it before you think it.

A tightening. A leaning forward. A readiness.

You begin constructing your response while they are still speaking.

You tell yourself you care about truth. You tell yourself clarity matters. You tell yourself bad ideas should not go unchallenged.

Sometimes that is true.

But sometimes something else is happening.

Arguing is often an attempt to resolve inner unease through outer dominance.

Difference can feel destabilizing. When someone holds a view that conflicts with yours, it subtly threatens your footing. If their view stands unchallenged, does that weaken yours? If you remain silent, does that imply agreement? If you do not correct them, does that mean you lack conviction?

So, you engage.

At work, it looks more polished. A colleague questions your proposal. You push back. They respond. You refine your argument. The exchange remains civil, but underneath it is something sharper.

You are not merely exploring ideas.
You are defending territory.

Because when disagreement appears, it can feel personal.

Your ideas are not separate from you. They represent your intelligence, your values, your discernment.

When someone challenges them, it can feel like a challenge to you.

The mind becomes a courtroom, and we argue the case again and again.

Evidence is presented. Counterarguments are sharpened. Weaknesses are exposed. And the goal, whether admitted or not, is victory.

Even when the argument is framed as discussion.

Even when the tone remains respectful.

Needing to be right is rarely worth what it costs.

At first, arguing can feel energizing. The mind sharpens. Language becomes precise. There is a sense of movement, of momentum.

But afterward, something lingers.

Arguing rarely ends at the table.
It continues internally.

Why?

Because beneath many arguments is a fear few people name.
The fear of being irrelevant.

If your ideas are dismissed, are you dismissed?
If your reasoning is flawed, are you diminished?
If you concede a point, have you surrendered something essential?

These questions may not be conscious.

But they influence tone.

Sometimes you argue not because the issue matters deeply, but because losing footing feels diminishing.

Certainty provides stability. Ambiguity destabilizes.

And so, urgency appears.

Urgency says:

This must be resolved now.
This must be corrected.
This cannot stand.

But not every disagreement requires resolution.
Not every difference requires collapse into sameness.
Two people can hold opposing views and remain intact.

The difficulty is not intellectual.
It's personal.

The ego prefers solidity. It prefers dominance over ambiguity. It prefers coherence over tension.
So, it moves to close the gap.

If you look carefully, you may notice that arguing often intensifies when you feel uncertain internally. When you are grounded, disagreement feels less threatening. When you are unsettled, disagreement feels sharper.

Arguing can become a way to reassure yourself that you still know where you stand.

But over time, habitual arguing reshapes relationships.

People grow cautious around you. Conversations narrow. Topics become landmines. Others may choose silence rather than engagement.

Not because you are wrong.
But because the cost of disagreement feels too high.

And something else happens internally.

When you are frequently in argument mode, you begin scanning for error. You listen for flaws more than meaning. You prepare rebuttals before curiosity.

That posture limits learning.

Because if your primary orientation is correction, you miss nuance.
You may win the moment but lose connection.

There is another way to inhabit disagreement.

You can hold your perspective without defending it against every opposing one.
You can say, "That's not how I see it," and allow the difference to remain.
You can ask questions not to expose weakness, but to understand how the other person arrived there.
You can remain internally steady even when the room does not align.

This is not passivity.
It is strength without urgency.

The difference is subtle but profound.

When urgency drives arguing, the goal is to eliminate tension.

When steadiness guides engagement, the goal is to explore without collapse.

Over time, you notice something surprising.

You do not need to win to remain whole.
You do not need to dominate to remain intelligent.
You do not need to close every gap to remain grounded.

In fact, allowing space between differing views can expand you.

It softens identity. It loosens rigidity. It increases range.

And perhaps most importantly, it changes the emotional climate of your relationships.

When others sense that disagreement does not automatically trigger contest, they relax.

Conversations widen.
Curiosity returns.
And something deeper than being right becomes possible.

Connection.

Needing to be right is rarely worth what it costs.

But being steady in difference – that changes everything.

CHAPTER 5

Fixing

Fixing relieves your tension,

even when it doesn't relieve theirs

Fixing rarely feels intrusive.

It feels helpful.

Someone you care about is struggling. A child is frustrated with homework. A spouse is overwhelmed. A friend calls late at night, discouraged and confused.

You listen for a moment.

Then you begin offering solutions.

Maybe the suggestions are practical. Maybe they're thoughtful. Maybe they're wise. You have experience. You have perspective. You want to reduce their burden.

Sometimes your help is welcome.

But sometimes something else is driving your impulse.

You are not only responding to their discomfort. You're responding to your own.

Watching someone struggle can feel intolerable.

When your child is frustrated, their distress lands in your body. When your partner feels stuck, you feel the weight with them. When a friend circles the same problem again and again, you feel the frustration building.

Helplessness is uncomfortable.

Fixing relieves your tension, even when it doesn't relieve theirs.

If you can solve it, the discomfort ends – for both of you.

Or so it seems.

You're sitting at the kitchen table. Your child pushes the paper away.
"I can't do this."

You feel the urge immediately. You lean forward. You begin guiding, correcting, restructuring the problem. You speak quickly, efficiently.

You are trying to help.

But perhaps you are also trying to eliminate the discomfort of watching them struggle.

Sometimes struggle is not a problem to be solved, but a process unfolding.
When you rush to fix, you interrupt that process.

With adults, it's more subtle.

A friend shares the same frustration for the third time. You've already offered advice. They haven't taken it. You feel irritation rising – not only at the problem, but at them for not doing what you suggested.

So, you sharpen your recommendation. You insist gently. You emphasize what they "should" do.

You tell yourself you're being honest.
But underneath that insistence may be a quiet impatience:

Why won't this resolve? Why won't they listen?

Sometimes fixing carries a subtle form of superiority.

If I see the solution clearly, why can't you?

That thought may never be spoken. But it shapes tone.

Fixing can become a way of stabilizing your own sense of competence.
You become the capable one. The steady one. The resourceful one.

And that role can feel good.

But over time, it can reshape the relationship.

When you habitually fix, others may stop exploring out loud. They may withhold vulnerability, anticipating correction. They may begin to feel slightly inadequate in your presence.

Not because you intended harm.
But because urgency entered the interaction.

Urgency says:

This must be solved.
This discomfort must end.
This problem cannot linger.

But growth takes time.

Clarity takes time.

Insight rarely arrives under pressure.

When you rush to fix, you may relieve immediate tension – but you also remove the space where resilience develops.

Helplessness is difficult to tolerate.

It challenges your sense of usefulness. It challenges your identity as someone who contributes. It challenges your control.

If you're not solving, what are you offering?

This is where the habit deepens into identity.

"I am the one who helps."
"I am the one who solves."
"I am the one who knows what to do."

Those identities are admirable.

But when driven by urgency, they become compulsive.

You begin scanning for problems you can address.
You feel restless when nothing needs intervention.
You interpret silence as inefficiency.

And gradually, relationships become subtly transactional.
Your value becomes tied to your utility.

But presence does not require utility.

Sometimes the most stabilizing thing you can offer another person is not a solution – but steadiness.

Sitting with someone while they struggle is uncomfortable.
It exposes your own limits.
It forces you to accept that you cannot manage every outcome.

But it also communicates something powerful:

I trust you to move through this.
I do not need to rescue you in order to remain connected to you.

When fixing softens, listening deepens.

When urgency eases, patience expands.

You still help when help is invited.
You still intervene when intervention is necessary.
But you stop equating action with care.

You allow space.

And in that space, something unexpected often emerges.

People find their own clarity.

Children discover their own capabilities.

Friends articulate insights they would not have reached if you had solved the problem too quickly.

Fixing relieves your tension.
But restraint builds strength – in both of you.

Over time, you realize that not every struggle requires your hand.

Some require your presence.
And presence is not passive.

It is steady.

CHAPTER 6

Not Doing

The quiet power of leaving things alone

You may have noticed something unsettling as you read.

If defending, explaining, arguing, and fixing are often driven by urgency, then much of what feels like maturity may actually be compulsion.

We learn to respond.

We are praised for responsiveness. We are valued for engagement. We are told that good communication requires articulation, correction, intervention.

Very few of us are taught the discipline of restraint.

Not suppression.

Restraint.

There is a difference.

You're in a conversation. Someone makes a comment that slightly misrepresents what you meant. You feel the familiar tightening. The opening forms in your mouth – the clarification ready to arrive.

But this time, you do not speak.
You let the sentence pass.
The discomfort spikes.

For a moment, you feel exposed. Mis-seen. Off balance.
Your mind argues: This needs correction.

But you wait.

The conversation continues.
No catastrophe follows.

That small moment contains more power than it appears.
There is a space between what happens and what you do next.

That space is not theoretical.

It is physical.

It lives in your breath.
It lives in the pause before you interrupt.

It lives in the half-second where you decide whether to add another explanation.

And in that space, urgency reveals itself.

Urgency does not always shout.

Sometimes it's subtle and persuasive:

Say something.
Fix this.
Clarify that.
Don't let this stand.

Urgency exaggerates consequence.

It convinces you that silence equals weakness, that non-response equals agreement or surrender, that restraint equals disengagement.

But most moments are not emergencies.
Most conversations do not hinge on your immediate intervention.
Most misunderstandings soften without repair.

Stillness is active restraint.

It is not passive.

It is strength without agitation.

When you experiment with not doing, the first thing you encounter is discomfort.

You feel useless.

If I am not correcting, what am I contributing?
If I am not explaining, what am I protecting?
If I am not solving, what am I offering?

For many people, identity is built around usefulness.

"I am the one who knows."
"I am the one who clarifies."
"I am the one who resolves tension."

There is something deeper beneath that usefulness.
A quiet fear most of us rarely name.

Not fear of harm.
Fear of being diminished.
Fear of being mis-seen.
Unnecessary.
Wrong.
Irrelevant.
Replaceable.
Invisible.

In short – fear of losing who you are.

Urgency is what that fear feels like when something about you seems at stake.

Urgency is fear mobilized.

It's fear moving into action.
It just doesn't feel like fear.

When you defend, it's because something in you feels threatened.
When you explain, something in you feels misunderstood.
When you argue, something in you feels destabilized.
When you fix, something in you feels unnecessary.

The reflex is not weakness.
It's protection.

You are not flawed.
You are protecting something you believe must remain intact.

And when you realize that what you are protecting is rarely in true danger, the guarding can soften.

When you stop reacting, you may notice a strange sensation.

You feel less defined.

If you are not correcting, who are you?
If you are not clarifying, who are you?
If you are not solving, who are you?

For many people, response has become identity.

You feel solid when you are needed.

So, when you choose not to respond, even for a moment, there is a flicker of emptiness.

It can feel like fading.

That is rarely named.
But it's common.

Much of urgency is a strategy against that fading.

If you are active, you are visible.
If you are correcting, you are significant.
If you are solving, you are necessary.

Not doing can feel like disappearing.

But what actually disappears is not you.

It's the role.

And when the role softens, something steadier can emerge.

You're still here.

Not because you acted.

But because you are.

That realization changes everything.

You do not need constant reaction to prove your existence.

You do not need perpetual intervention to justify your place in the room.

You do not need urgency to feel real.

When you see that clearly, relief comes quietly.

You are allowed to be present without performing.

You are allowed to care without controlling.

You are allowed to exist without constantly responding.

That is not passivity.

Stillness

From stillness, steadiness emerges.

And steadiness does not rush.

When you stop responding automatically, you temporarily release that identity.

That can feel destabilizing.

Without the reflex to manage, you must sit with uncertainty.

Without the reflex to correct, you must tolerate imperfection.

Without the reflex to fix, you must witness struggle.

Helplessness is uncomfortable.

Ambiguity is uncomfortable.

Misinterpretation is uncomfortable.

But discomfort is not the same as danger.

Urgency confuses the two.

When you do not intervene, something subtle shifts inside you.

You begin to notice how often your previous actions were attempts to regulate internal tension rather than serve the moment.

You notice how frequently your body reacted before your mind had discerned.
You notice how much of your identity depended on being the one who responded.
And you begin to see that life continues without your constant management.

A conversation moves forward without your correction.
A misunderstanding resolves without your explanation.
A disagreement fades without your argument.
A problem resolves without your solution.

Life requires far less management than we assume.

That realization can feel both liberating and humbling.
You are not indispensable to every ripple.
You are not responsible for every shift in tone.
You are not required to stabilize every disturbance.

Over time, something else emerges.

Not indifference.

Not withdrawal.

Trust.

Trust that you can remain steady without dominating the moment.
Trust that others can navigate their own discomfort.
Trust that ambiguity can exist without collapsing connection.
Trust that your value does not depend on constant intervention.

This trust is quiet.

It does not announce itself.
It appears as breath deepening.
As shoulders lowering.
As conversations feeling lighter.
As energy conserved.

The quiet power of not doing is this:

You are no longer compelled.

You are no longer governed by internal alarms that mistake friction for threat.

You begin to respond from discernment rather than urgency.

You still speak.
You still help.
You still engage.

But you choose – rather than react.

And in that choosing, something inside you rests for the first time in a long while.

When you see urgency clearly, something in you is revealed.

You begin to notice how much of your effort was protection.
How much of your engagement was self-definition.
How much of your speed was fear disguised as responsibility.

Seeing that is not condemning.

It is clarifying.

And clarity brings relief.

You do not have to carry every moment.
You do not have to repair every ripple.
You do not have to prove your worth through response.

As the pressure eases, understanding deepens.

You begin to recognize the pattern in yourself – and in others.
You see how often reaction masquerades as strength.
You see how much steadiness requires restraint.

That understanding feels like light entering a room that was already familiar – but dim.

And with that light comes a quiet sense of power.

Not power over others.

Power over compulsion.
The power to pause.
The power to choose.
The power to remain steady.

Revealed.
Relieved.
Enlightened.
Empowered.

Not by adding something new.
But by releasing what was unnecessary.

Restraint matures into steadiness.

Steadiness matures into presence.

And nowhere is that steadiness tested more quickly than in relationships.

Presence does not need to hurry.

CHAPTER 7

Relationships

Where Fear Is Most Exposed

Most of these habits were learned in relationships.

They did not develop in isolation.
They developed where connection mattered.

And if fear of losing who you are sits beneath urgency, then nowhere does that fear surface more quickly than in relationships.

A stranger's comment may irritate you.
But a spouse's disagreement can feel destabilizing.

A colleague's critique can feel threatening.
A child's resistance can feel personal.

The closer someone is to you, the more their perception touches identity.

You are rarely wounded by those who do not matter.
It's the people you love who can unsettle you most.

Not because they are harsher.

But because their perception reaches further inside.

Closeness magnifies significance.

And significance magnifies vulnerability.

You do not defend most fiercely where stakes are low.

You defend where you feel seen. Or mis-seen.

Relationships are mirrors.

And mirrors are rarely neutral.

When someone close to you misunderstands your intention, something in you tightens.

When someone questions your judgment, something in you flares.

When someone struggles and does not take your advice, something in you feels dismissed.

It is not simply the moment.

It's what the moment seems to say about you.

Am I respected?

Am I valued?

Am I necessary?

Am I understood?

That is why these habits are most visible at home – with the people you love most.

Because love makes identity vulnerable.

If I stop defending, will I disappear in this relationship?
If I stop explaining, will I be overlooked?
If I stop arguing, will I lose ground?
If I stop fixing, will I lose relevance?

These are rarely conscious thoughts.
They move beneath the surface.
And urgency rises to defend.

When you begin to see this, something shifts.

Not immediately in the other person.

In you.

You realize that much of your engagement was not about solving the moment.
It was about securing your place within it.

That realization can feel uncomfortable.

Because it means the tension was not entirely theirs.

It was shared.

And yet, that discomfort is clarifying.

When you stop protecting identity in the moment, relationships change.

Not because conflict disappears.

But because you are no longer defending who you are inside it.

When you stop defending, others feel less opposed.
When you stop explaining, others feel less managed.
When you stop arguing, others feel less cornered.
When you stop fixing, others feel less diminished.

This does not guarantee harmony.

There will still be disagreement.

There will still be misunderstanding.

There will still be difference.

But the emotional charge softens.

Without reflexes, relationships gain space.

Space for listening instead of preparing rebuttal.
Space for curiosity instead of correction.
Space for people to be unfinished without being repaired.

You begin to notice something subtle.

You are no longer responsible for stabilizing every fluctuating tone.

You can show up without steering.
Care without managing.
Love without controlling.

Not reacting does not mean not caring.

It means caring without the illusion of control.

And when you release that illusion, something surprising happens.

Others step forward.

When they are not being corrected, they think more carefully.
When they are not being rescued, they grow more capable.
When they are not being argued with, they soften.

And if they do not, you learn something equally important. You learn where your influence ends.

That boundary is not failure.

It's clarity.

And clarity brings a different kind of connection – one built not on urgency, but on presence.

Presence does not perform.
It does not persuade.
It does not rescue.

It stays.

Over time, relationships shaped by presence feel lighter.

There is more room for humor.

More room for truth.

More room for silence.

And you begin to trust that connection does not require constant effort.

It requires steadiness.

And space.

CHAPTER 8

Becoming

Who you become when urgency no longer leads

By the time you begin softening defending, explaining, arguing, and fixing, something unexpected begins to shift.

You do not simply behave differently.

You begin to become someone different.

Urgency shapes personality more than we realize.

What you repeatedly protect becomes who you appear to be.

Over time, you begin to mistake the protection for the self.

You believe you are decisive when you are braced.
You believe you are articulate when you are anxious.
You believe you are helpful when you are afraid to be unnecessary.

And so, the posture hardens.

Not because it's true. But because it's rehearsed.

If you are frequently defending, you become guarded.
If you are frequently explaining, you become over-articulate and cautious.
If you are frequently arguing, you become sharp and vigilant.
If you are frequently fixing, you become indispensable – and slightly restless.

Over time, these habits do not just appear in moments.

They define posture.

They influence tone.

They shape how others experience you.

They shape how you experience yourself.

You may have been described as:

Intense.
Capable.
Strong-willed.

Helpful.

Precise.

None of those are flaws.

But when urgency fuels them, they harden.

And hardness limits range.

When urgency softens, identity softens.

You begin to move differently.

Leadership shifts.

A leader without urgency does not rush to correct publicly.

They do not react to every challenge as threat.

They do not mistake dissent for disloyalty.

They listen longer.

They speak slower.

They allow silence.

And paradoxically, authority increases.

Because steadiness is magnetic.

Parenting shifts.

Instead of intervening at the first sign of struggle, you observe.
Instead of correcting tone immediately, you breathe.
Instead of solving frustration instantly, you allow capacity to build.

Children feel trusted rather than managed.

They sense that you are not threatened by their emotions.

Marriage shifts.

Conversations lose edge.
Disagreements are shorter because urgency does not escalate them.
Misunderstandings do not spiral because they are not over-managed.

There is less tightening.

Less scorekeeping.

More space.

Even your inner life changes.

The constant rehearsal of conversations quiets.
The mental courtroom dissolves.
The imagined arguments fade.
The urge to refine explanations at 2 a.m. lessens.

Your nervous system stabilizes.

You are no longer preparing to defend or rehearsing how to clarify.
You are no longer managing perception in every exchange.

There is room for thought without agitation.
Room for curiosity without combat.
Room for care without control.

And something else becomes visible.

When urgency softens, humility increases.

You do not need to be right as often.

You do not need to be understood perfectly.

You do not need to solve every problem.

That humility does not weaken you. It expands you.

Because rigidity consumes energy.
Flexibility conserves it.

Over time, you begin to recognize that much of your earlier intensity was self-protective.

You were managing risk.
Managing perception.
Managing emotional climate.
Managing outcomes.

But life does not require constant management.

It requires presence.

Presence without urgency feels different.

It's slower.

Not lazy.

Steadier.

It's attentive without being reactive.

Engaged without being agitated.

Caring without controlling.

You may notice that conversations feel lighter around you.

Not because you withdraw.

But because others feel less braced.

They do not anticipate correction.

They do not anticipate argument.

They do not anticipate immediate solution.

They experience steadiness.

And steadiness is rare.

The world rewards speed, correction, certainty, intervention.

But wisdom often looks like restraint.

You may speak less.

But your words carry more weight.

You may act less.

But your actions feel deliberate.

You may intervene less.

But when you do, it matters.

This is not self-improvement.

It's self-simplification.

You are not adding skills.

You are shedding compulsion.

And in that shedding, something truer emerges.

Not a better version of you.

A steadier one.

Becoming someone who is not driven by urgency changes more than conversations.

It changes the quality of your presence in your own life.

CHAPTER 9

A Way of Seeing

This book does not offer a method

It offers a way of seeing

Once you see the reflex to defend, explain, argue, and fix, you cannot unsee it.

You begin to notice it everywhere - not just in yourself, but in the world.

You see how much noise comes from urgency.
How much conflict comes from fear.
How much exhaustion comes from trying to manage life.

Seeing does not require correction.

You don't need to stop these habits completely.
You don't need to replace them with better ones.

You only need to notice.

Notice when you reach.
Notice what you fear would happen if you didn't.
Notice how often nothing truly requires your response.

This noticing shifts the quality of your presence.

You listen more.
You interrupt less.
You allow moments to complete themselves.

Life becomes quieter – not because there is less happening, but because there is less interference.

There is a freedom in this.

The moment before reaction is the moment we are most free.

Freedom from needing to be right.
From needing to be understood.
From needing to be useful at every moment.

You discover that you can be misunderstood and still be okay.

You can disagree and remain connected.
You can watch others struggle and not rush in.

This is not detachment.

It is trust.

Trust in yourself.
Trust in others.
Trust in life's ability to unfold without constant supervision.

When the need to be heard softens, more is heard.
When the need for control loosens, there is greater steadiness.
When the need to fix relaxes, there is more closeness.

Presence

You don’t need to be right.

Understood.

Or useful at every moment.

The world does not need constant response.

The world responds to presence.

And presence begins where effort ends.

○

Acknowledgments

This book did not come from certainty, but from noticing what happens in lived experience.

I'm grateful to the many teachers who helped me learn when effort was unnecessary, when silence was wiser than response, and when presence carried more truth than explanation.

I owe thanks to those whose lives and work pointed quietly to these truths long before I had language for them, and to those whose example reminded me that wisdom is often lived rather than taught.

I'm especially grateful to the people who allow me to be unfinished in their presence. Your patience, honesty, and restraint shaped this work more than you know.

Much of what is written here was not discovered so much as recognized.

And finally, thank you, reader – for slowing down, for pausing, and for trusting what does not need to be defended. If any part of this work proves useful, it will not be because it taught something new, but because it helped something familiar become visible again.

www.ingramcontent.com/pod-product-compliance
Ingram Content Group UK Ltd.
Pitfield, Milton Keynes, MK11 3LW, UK
UKHW041046300726
14061UKWH00008BA/94

9 798995 423201